Ultimate
Home & Interior Design
Vision Board

Clip Art & Picture Book

Over 300 Pictures & Affirmations

Welcome to the world of Vision Boarding
where if YOU can SEE it,
YOU can ACHIEVE it.

A Vision Board is a carefully curated combination of words, images and concepts that speak to you and where you want to go. Creating a Vision Board is very personal and particular to you. After all, it's a visual representation of YOUR goals and vision for YOUR life journey.

Once you've arranged your Vision Board, it will give you a tangible reminder every day of the life you aspire to, and, the life that you're inspired to live.

Making a Vision Board is easy. Here are a few tips to get you started on your journey.

1. Cut out any words and images that you like. You can use scissors, an exacto knife or even carefully tear out the image or words you want to use. Don't think too hard about this, just go with what inspires you to live your best life.

2. Arrange the images and words on a canvas made up of a piece of paper, an art board, a wood panel, a journal or anything that you know you'll be able to put in a place where you will reference it daily.

3. Attach the images and words to your canvas and stick them down with glue or tape.

4. Use colored pens or pencils, stickers, glitter or other fun and creative ways to further personalize your Vision Board.

5. Put your Vision Board in a place where you'll see it often. If you can see it, you can achieve it!

I hope this book gives you lots of images, words and ideas to help guide you to where you want to go and what you want to do on this journey of life. DREAM BIG! I'm rooting for you!!!

Sarah

Design Fearlessly

Create Your Cozy Space

DESIGN YOUR DREAMS

Embrace Your World

DISCOVER CREATIVITY

DIP YOUR TOES IN DESIGN

DIP YOUR TOES IN DESIGN

CREATE YOUR SPACE

Freedom to Choose

experience something new

experience something new

PRACTICE GRATITUDE

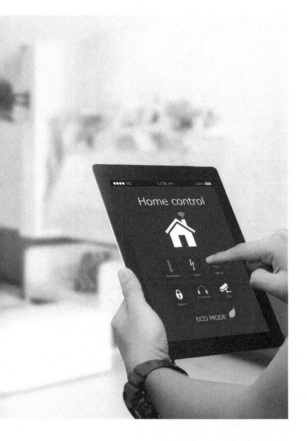

BE YOU NO MATTER
WHERE YOU ARE

Be Open to Change

Surround Yourself With Joy

EMBRACE THE ARTIST IN YOU

EMBRACE THE ARTIST IN YOU

keep a journal

keep a journal

GET BUSY CREATING

TRUST YOUR EYE

Experience Life Fearlessly

Experience Life Fearlessly

Let Yourself Be Free

Let Yourself Be Free

DESIGN YOUR LIFE

DESIGN YOUR LIFE

Reach for Your Dreams

NEVER STOP LEARNING

Discover Yourself

Rearrange the Furniture

Rearrange the Furniture

Go for IT!

Go for IT!

USE FRESH FLOWERS

HONOR YOURSELF

HONOR YOURSELF

WALK THE PATH UNTAKEN

tilt your head

all your head

You Have Permission

find inspiration everywhere

ENJOY ALL THE LITTLE THINGS

ENJOY ALL THE LITTLE THINGS

Make Bold Moves

Make Bold Moves

TALK WITH YOUR FRIENDS

TALK WITH YOUR FRIENDS

CELEBRATE THE SMALL THINGS

ask for advice

don't be afraid to knock down walls

don't be afraid to knock
down walls

ALLOW YOURSELF TO GROW

Find Your Fuel

Find Your Fuel

MAKE COURAGEOUS CHOICES

DO WHAT YOU LOVE

Make Your Plan

display the weird stuff

display the weird stuff

REMEMBER YOU

If you're on a path you don't like
Change Direction

PAINT WITH COLORS

enjoy where you are

enjoy where you are

Face the Unknown with Fear

Face the Unknown with Fear

Share Your World

DO WHAT YOU WANT TO DO

DO WHAT YOU WANT TO DO